LEI NECKLACE

The necklace is made up of several links, from an even number of dollar bills. It can be made in any length.

1A. Valley fold the right edge up about 1/4 inch (1/2 cm)
1B. Mountain fold the left edge to the BACK about 1/4 inch (1/2 cm)

2A. Fold the bill in half lengthwise. Unfold this crease.
2B. Fold both long edges to the middle.

3. Roll the paper and slide one end into the other. The edge with the cuff on the outside slides inside the other edge. This locks the chain link.

4. One completed link.

How to interlock links:
Slide the second link through the first one, before locking it in step 4. Add more links in the same way.

Colored links
If you want to make a chain with a set amount of money, you can still make it as long as you like by adding a few links made from colored paper, cut to the size of dollar bills.

1

2

4

3

FLIPOVER FROG

Begin with the President's face up.

1. Fold the bottom side up about 1 inch (2.5cm)

2. At the top fold the short edge to the long edge, creasing through the middle of the corner. Unfold this crease.

3. At the same end, fold the short edge to the other long edge. Unfold. You will have made an X on the paper.

4. Fold to the BACK (mountain fold) right through the middle of the X.

5. Now all creases are in place for the next tricky move. Flip the short back flap over to the front. Push down at the middle of the X. Push the short edges down, forming a triangle on the front.

STEP 5 IN PROGRESS   STEP 5 COMPLETED

6. Fold the outside corners of the triangle to the top corner. They will be the front legs of the frog.

7. Fold the sides of the bill to meet in the middle. The slanted edges line up neatly next to the front legs.

8. Fold the bottom edge to the top.

9. Fold the same edge down.

10. The Flipover Frog is completed. To make it flip over, loosen the front and back legs a little, stand it up and tap the frog smartly on the back edge.

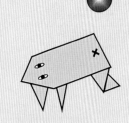

6

7

8

9

10

TAP
HERE

FLOWER DECORATION

As little surprise gifts leave money flowers in unexpected places. Or tape one or more flowers, with or without leaves, on a gift package.

You need
Two dollar bills
A wire twist
Cellophane tape
A thin straw (or floral wire or thin dowel), 6 in (15 cm)
Green floral stem wrap tape (optional)

Flower

1. Crease narrow pleats all across one of the bills.

2. Hold the pleats tightly in a bundle and tie the wire twist across the middle. Fan out the pleats into a circle. Tape the raw edges together where they meet.

3. Completed Flower.

1

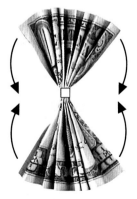

2

3

TAPED   TAPED

Leaves

1. Place the other bill with the President's face up.
Fold it in half lengthwise. Unfold.
Fold the four corners to the crease.

2. Fold the four slanted edges to the middle.

3. Fold the bottom corner up to the top corner.

4. Fold the bill in half.

5. Reach inside and pull the hidden leaf out.

6. Completed Leaves.

Assembly

Attach a straw with the wire twist which is already on the flower. If you like, you can wind floral tape around the straw first. Slide the other end of the straw into the leaves and tape it inside.

Table favors

For individual table favors you can create standing flowers. Before taping in the stem, fold the bottom corners out to make a stand. Then tape in the stem and staple the bottom corners to a small, heavy cardboard square.

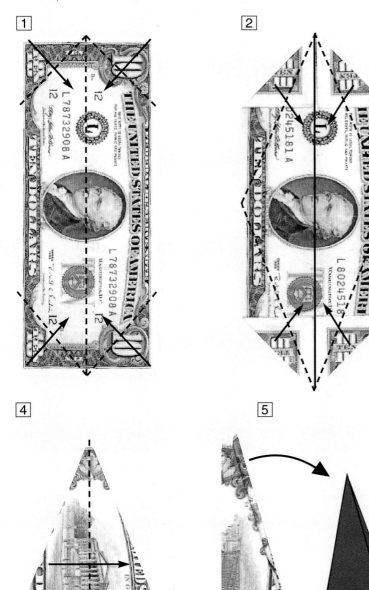

1

2

3

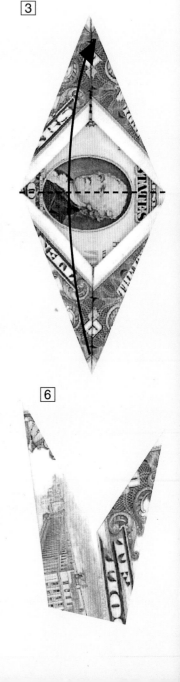

4

5

6

PEACOCK

The Peacock is a beautiful design which excites a lot of admiration, but includes some tricky moves. It's best to attempt it after you have folded some easier things in this book. When you have folded the peacock once or twice you'll probably be able to fold it quickly to the amazement of your friends and strangers.

1. Fold the bill in half iengthwise. Unfold it.
Fold two corners to the middle crease.

2. Fold the slanted edges to the middle crease.

3A. Fold down the tip of the paper to make the beak later on.

3B. Mountain fold to the BACK on line A-B. Then make parallel pleats up and down (valley and mountain folds) for the rest of the flat part of the paper.

4. TURN OVER FRONT TO BACK.

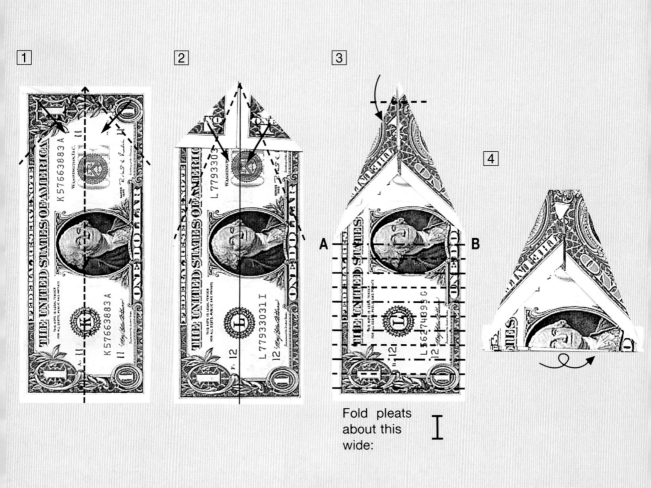

Fold pleats about this wide: I

5. Fold the top edge down to lie next to the pleats.

6. TURN OVER BACK TO FRONT

7. Fold the top edge to the bottom edge. Note that the back layer is not folded but swings up. See next illustration.

8. Mountain fold to the BACK.

9. Hold at X and pull at Y until the slanted back edges line up with the bottom edge.

10. Pull the neck forward and crease at the bottom to make the neck stay in place. Pull the head forward and crease it at the back to make it stay. Spread the pleats a little.

11. Completed Peacock.

Tail up

A male peacock opens its tail when it wants to show off. You can show off your Peacock by raising up the pleats. First glue or tape the edges at the middle of the fan. Then push the fan upright. If you want to keep the tail up, place a piece of double - sided tape between the body and the fan.

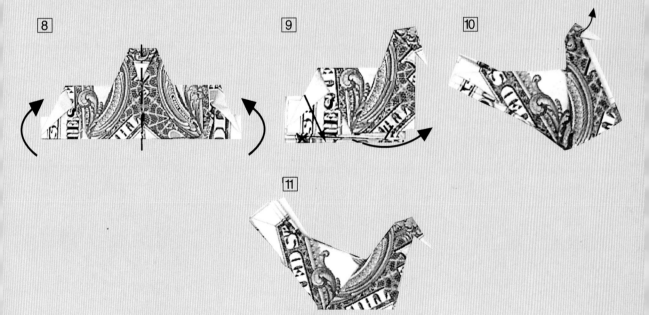

VERSATILE EARRINGS

With a few quick twists you can turn dollar bills into a pair of bold earrings - or an informal tie, a hair ornament, a tip in a restaurant or other amusing giveaways.

The instructions show how to twist a money bill into the basic earring and are followed by suggestions how to make other versatile things.

1. Fold a bill in half lengthwise.

2. Fold it in half again. You will have a narrow strip.

3. Measure 2 inch (5 cm) along the top edge and crease the strip down.

1

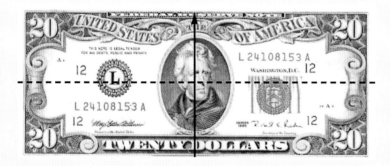

2

3

2" (5cm)

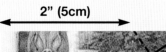

4. Fold the strip to the left.

5. Fold the strip up and tuck it under.

6. Place the earring with the two ends facing down.

7. Fold the four outside corners to the BACK (mountain folds).

8. Versatile Earring.

A Pair of Earrings
Make two versatile earrings.
For pierced ears: At the top of each earring make a hole with a pin.
For unpierced ears: Insert earring clips on the back, sliding them under the top corners. Glue them with Duco cement.
(Earring loops and clips are sold in craft stores.)

More Ideas
Turn a folded earring into an Easter Rabbit by adding whiskers and eyes. Or glue two folded earrings sideways on a greeting card to look like fish swimming. For a special prize medal glue an earring to a blue circle. And just for fun wear one as a hair bow or as a tie on a shirt.

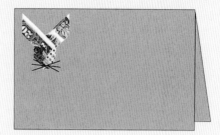

4

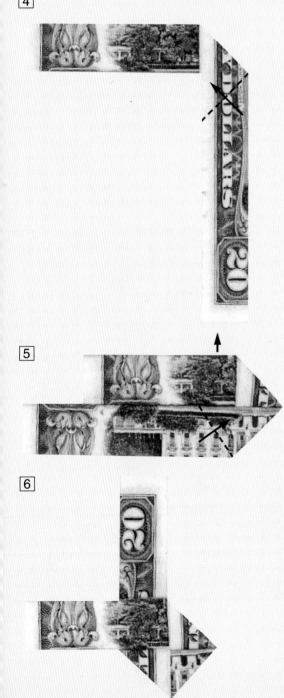

5

6

7

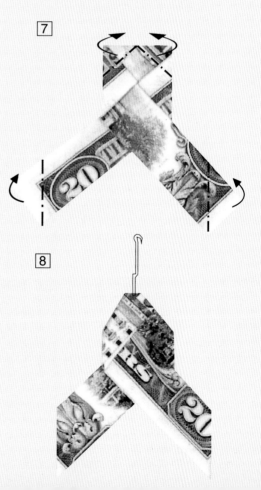

8

CROW PUPPET

When this puppet opens and shuts its mouth, you can imagine it to be a crow or any other animal or personality. It's a wonderful toy for storytellers or for brightening up a long wait in a doctor's office. For a party give every guest a puppet to help along the singing of "Happy Birthday."

For a black crow begin with the green side of the bill facing up.

1. Fold the bill in half lengthwise. Unfold.

2. Fold the four corners to the middle crease.

3. Fold the four slanted edges to the middle crease.

4. Fold the bill in half the short way.

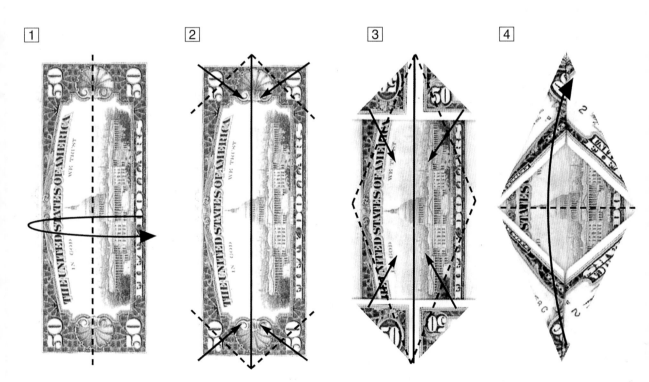

5. Fold down the top corner, front flap only.

6. Fold the slanted edges A-B and B-C to lie along the horizontal middle line. See next illustration.

7. Unfold step 6.

8. Repeat step 6 on the right side, bringing the slanted edges (AD-DC) to the horizontal middle line.

9. Fold the right side of the Crow in half to the BACK (mountain fold) on the middle line. At the same time let the beak swing out to the right and settle into the creases made in steps 6 and 8.

10. Completed Crow Puppet. You can open and shut the beak by moving the sides apart at the Xs.

5

6

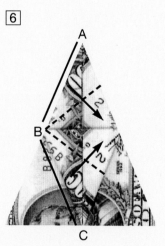

7

8

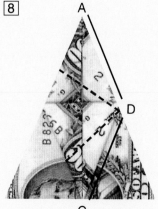

9

10

MONEY FOLDING TIPS

Money Magic:

Become a magician when you fold money for your friends or relatives. If you want to raise funds for a cause, you can charge a premium for folded money items.

Sharp Creases:

Crisp, new dollar bills give the best results. It helps to go over creases with a ruler or popsicle stick.

Temporary Glues:

You can attach folded money bills to cards and wrapped gifts with rubber cement, temporary glue sticks or double-sided sticky tape. Any residue can be rubbed off easily, and the bills can then be unfolded and used.

Gifts:

A greeting card can become a gift when you attach a folded bill to a piece of paper folded in half. It's a welcome way to give presents for birthdays, Christmas, Hanukkah, Kwanzaa, New Year and other occasions.

Currencies:

Argentina:	Peso	Hungary:	Forint	Poland:	Zloty
Australia:	Dollar	India:	Rupee	Portugal:	Escudo
Austria:	Schilling	Indonesia:	Rupiah	Russia:	Ruble
Belgium:	Franc	Iran:	Rial	Saudi Arabia:	Riyal
Brazil	Real	Ireland:	Punt	Singapore:	Dollar
Britain:	Pound	Israel:	Shekel	Slovak Rep:	Koruna
Canada:	Dollar	Italy:	Lira	South Africa:	Rand
Chile:	Peso	Japan:	Yen	South Korea:	Won
Columbia:	Peso	Jordan:	Dinar	Spain:	Peseta
Czech Rep:	Koruna	Lebanon:	Pound	Sweden:	Korna
Denmark	Korne	Malaysia:	Ringgit	Switzerland:	Franc
Ecuador:	Sucre	Mexico	Peso	Taiwan:	NT $
Egypt:	Pound	Netherlands:	Guilder	Thailand:	Baht
Finland:	Mark	New Zealand:	Dollar	Turkey:	Lira
France:	Franc	Norway:	Krone	U.A.E.:	Dirham
Germany:	Mark	Pakistan:	Rupee	Uruguay	New Peso
Greece:	Drachma	Peru:	New Sol	Venezuela:	Bolivar
Hong Kong:	Dollar	Philippines:	Peso		